GREAT GUNS

FARNOOSH FATHI

CANARIUM BOOKS
ANN ARBOR, STUTTGART, IOWA CITY

SPONSORED BY
THE UNIVERSITY OF MICHIGAN
CREATIVE WRITING PROGRAM

GREAT GUNS

Canarium Books
Ann Arbor, Marfa, Iowa City
www.canarium.org

The editors gratefully acknowledge the
University of Michigan Helen Zell Writers' Program
for editorial assistance and generous support.

Cover: Lynn Buckley

First Edition
Second Printing

Printed in the United States of America

ISBN 13: 978-0-9849471-1-9

to my parents

In the most startling atmospheric accidents,
A youthful couple holds itself aloof on the ark,
—Is it primitive shyness that people pardon?—
And sings and stands guard.

—Arthur Rimbaud, "Motion"

CONTENTS

I

II

III

* * *

Jimmy crack corn and I don't care.
Jimmy crack corn and I don't care.
A light peck cracks the constellation.
They want our secret without becoming like.
They want our secret to undo.
Jimmy crack corn and I don't care—
a pure harpoon dissolves in outer space.
Bone by bone, we have backed too far
in divulgence to frost with reticence,
nor do we look as happy as the indigenous.
Stars, we trusted you!

Brimming over a secret alone, the end
of its thought must be lost in a hum.
Jimmy crack corn and I don't care—
the waves explode but cannot kill a snail
whose castle is the quiet
on a nun's navel.

MEMORY

Over the night a bull
Whispers into a coal

:Unmeant in the stall to sit and plate,
But sixth, with all the senses,
To consume—
Incorporate—those signal
Impressions which are (we know) its fate:

In explosions, in hard strides,
His coattails fly; to bits, to friends
Craven and brave.

Sadness undulates at their back.

His lilt's a cotillion of flies.

But how he charges, he commits!

Each to the next.

It seems unfair, a target lies

Between its shoulder blades.

And another whisps right back:

A drop of blood would pin back his wild hair

Which wanders as it wills

A sunset like acupuncture

LETTER

So this breezy mystery bruise is also earth's! She reads on; the yellow gulls arc and link at her breast; winter cracks the whites of her eyes, strange shapes egress! Too easy to forget, and in no less than human fashion, grief leaks its combination. But she cries, "not for what I did not understand but that it was meant for me alone." He thinks of the sparrow on heels of lead, the black spill of elevators and ice. She wipes and weeps to her taste, but how fast, too fast, things rise! The meadows they made once, tops, over which chance angles light a clover. "That thicket horsetail rain which I polished as a child stands up to me now." His eyes do not bulge and yet, are large. He tests himself, a man who stands in the rain of bone marrow, in the rain of bone, in the rain. And the rain stands on end like him; it falls in tatters for her joy; on a horse too inhaled by the distance peppered with pure mills, in a letter now too far to be sent in haste.

THE CONDUCTOR

In winter when the music waned and only the fly unzipped
     silences
briefly in their ears, the conductor spoke
like a white crow emerged from a snowed-in head: These sad
     stones we skip make
infinite notes across the lake, and we are bound
to sound of what we throw so far, for no one sake.
Seizureless, among compact mirrors, black violets,
night rearranges the universe in her hair. The waves
pull the self-denying land
out from under one man's sleeping feet. He only
lets his feet dream. I am that man and these are my robes
that melt upon realization.

          A vision must turn on itself and wander,
in order to reckon a new earth,
while hearts may still be heard octagonally,
among cattails dreaming of birds dropping white violets
like ions loosed from outskirts. As the earth may be our best
     listener,
parting the grass of waking dreams,
that led us here and back again,
and back to let us hear again.
It is there now: a white noise it makes, like a fat cat in narrow
     peace.

We don't need proof—the storm that took the snail's roof
is meaning enough to ache—and we feel, if our thinking is too
     late,

born for an earth turning away—
But an almost unnaturally suspended chord waits in between
the wings of corners; any weight it has with us
comes to be played, suddenly, out of the common blue woodwork,
having nothing won we can't release to wind. And wheeling
    through likely lies
with such force are oldest birds
who will still shed feathers
in flight while dreaming, though later cold.

GREAT GUNS

Who goes, asked the pore, there on one hand so beautiful? The
    modern
nets and fishes out contumely; there is palsy in the grass high on
    noon's shoulders.
The great guns of a lover—
his sweat broke into ants that led the other way.
One must lie down. Grand debt of the observer!
This unremarkable suffering and these annotations on the lily.
Even the water here grows, spoken of, so highly, so likely.

It comes rolling on an eye
to a foothill and it stops; its drops stretch taut—like
the guts of heavens devising
to suck the ivy of visitors from even the safest face, behind which
a lover peels and peels; as certain and as full as all beauty, its obese
    gold navels
and indelible shoes without escape.

ANGEL BALLS

If I only knew what I knew then
First myself
Dressed in thunder's Sylvester

Robes—

My neighbor goes out
Your light sought out

The unconscious pearshaped in the fragrance
Garden, and these identical
That are to partake and brave the hole of this becoming shape,
Not stiff centered Monday, but the spheres I knew
Before the war you lengthened with your finger—

Not even with my dog-ear up and radar radar
Have I chosen; nor this snuff glossary you shine
Free of;
The same old ridden
Quintessence which is particular and
Guardian, a kite at last
The wind took to.

Innumerable exactitudes—
Nothing I can do, but I can also make heaven
Drip the standing dream—
Steep waiter

And steeper—
Drop Angel Ball Crater

APOLOGY

Air—this faceless currency—
That is why the gulf
She looked—and wrapped
For the injured worm
A dark maypole:

"Don't just be sour at my aim—
A small rock, a broken rib—prepare
For saints! If it's malady, this coursing cures
It, then cuts it out, and cured, preserves it.
Dark melody: a night light serves it.
Punch colors in peace place summer
At the pigeon's feet, that way, ways that a full ward cannot
When each is, asleep, a comet on a doily—
Stranger in place than not;

But not for the mo'—how it files
Into my mouth like glass
Like the beak of a lost messenger."
That is why they say she rose
Engrossed and fair—looked once,
Then folded back—a map like a wing to sleep.

SYMPATHY

Whose table is that, left on three legs?
If there's been a mistake, it may be
in assuming less vulnerability
as one fills the vase—

whose buoyant comfort exaggerates
at the sight of his own proffered,
sympathetic hand, striking him so clean
in comparison

gloved white, magician—
for a sec he even sees the calla lily's furl
in the gesture of voilà!

WORM RALLY

It is true, I must reverse it. I will slit in curves, distend mouth
    and rings,
  forcing my way, penitently with words—slither that—
now you see what I mean about words turning red, the hesitation

pushing the worm forward, consider this—the unseemly will of
    a creature
  that such pushing strength comes through it only as a hesitation
a slit-inch forward or back, making progress imperceptible.

The two signals the worm knows most frequent the earth
  are death and beauty, this gives its flesh
the life-long purpose of embedding spring, taut, the spine of
    spring

pulled out by gardeners—What pleasure in looking,
  even at the worm, especially at the living worm, one said
—as long as we know the worm's whys

because we are most bound to take pleasure in learning
  of any form, in understanding even
how to grip the squirm, vigilant and clean-beaked—

because it pleases that the mind can burrow anywhere,
  might snip this kingly sloth of rain puddles. This pleasure, said
another gardener, is analagous to the pleasure

derived from looking at a picture of the worm, that is if we
  can aim to understand why that was the best
way to capture the worm: lacquered or unflattered by proof

it leaves ten dozen crushed flash bulbs in the pure slime
  of its trail; to catch a fist of them throb in a cupid's
taut bow. So, I said to them, to know the underlying rationale

of the well-made thing can help the observer appreciate what
    snapped
  in the maker's mind? (Not clear whether it mattered if
a maker actually knew why, say, as stars coalesced beneath

the feet, they slipped right on like beaks; whether by instinct or
    error
  one has the pleasure of it not mattering, so long as it finally
catches.) Finally, when we sidle up to the worm, wind blares

and parallels. Worm and word, something so light and indefinite
  will never leave this circle. Now I said, I have been trying
to say the underlying even until now, but there is something

at the end of talking, gardeners—one feels something obviously
  forgotten and one begins to know its worth in perplexities,
starts to knock this air letting no one go until

foolishly (once will suffice) one has
  uncoiled into the embodied dumbstruck urges themselves,
and announces some undoing at the end so as to

preclude the end properly: Mystery = Wood = Wood
   because it is suddenly the floored and fist-stuttering matter—
alone with red/wing/blade the things that flap and give a worm
   its flying feel.

TWO HEAR CICADAS

BEEF: We are here between trees,
with the tempo of a rosary being strung
in a queue of escalating beads—

BEEF: It's not quite the count in
the countinghouse of my chest
but the heart does make an awful attempt

BEEF: a tee and a circle wherever it may
be there was music coming on

BEEF: which though machinery-like
moves not in cogs, and never
springs, but waves through

BEEF: like wired applause for antic backstage
buds on the pre-comeuppance buzz; but it
fades

BEEF: but only after the chorus has pulsed

BEEF: it drops off with sudden decision, like fountain
water gone dross

BEEF: or it reaches the furthest point
the branch turns from us, and is for some arc
fully quiet . . .

BEEF: until the roulette snaps its jaw and the choir's circuit opens to one

BEEF: like a pigeon unhinged, its wings in sudden white-rumped ascent

BEEF: unopposed by iridescence

BEEF: unopposed by iridescence

GOLD DOLT

A crescent cent shores up, a new name
in the drip-dry day. And you know, how granted some nucleus,
one glues the rest to toothpicks and standing back, looks to,
maybe mocks, the resultant gait: It will grow, some say,
    shrooming out of glare
like some golden dolt.
Go, I gut my way
to the choppy capitals of this mirror, and if I look behind me
and my shame is surmised, or it appears
I answer to shame—see that no point of my eye is insulated from
its greeny dead bolts and silken amplifications.
Each false step made a twist in the chains of his meats—
the peacock's.
(Like a confession burst from his silver vest came
"the pillow word for spring!" Or an expression knocked
from the boxer's face—an angel's "No.")

I am not free to overlook—he thinks,
There is some gentle perspectivist I am yet to meet
and thank;
without formula, she'll flush my marrow with a blow
and incline my vibratory illustrations toward
homes fat with children's practice.

HONEY/MANILA PORTFOLIO

This is not a book. Otherwise, by now
We would love each other.
You would not put me first,
Out of a kind habit, under your coat
And clutch—as a sudden rain
Spate down. For I've seen it done
For the hardly known.

No, you would know with a book you love:
How nothing held your eyes
The way the words did, with archer-focus:
How each arrow heading toward you
Was slowed by the dripping beehive
On its spike—

Nothing else could hold what you are
Still: I pressed your heart in speech and saw
What a musical you let rush, nothing
Else in the eyes. This is not a book,
But a streak—
Words cross reins—
The brow splits, veins careen.

APPROACHING A DRY-EYED WHALE

Into the eve of the beached the sun's cane pokes
The eye of the whale—"Set sail, set sail!

Once I was excused
From the table too. My talons sunk
The wood, to love. See that happy stray,
His tail is never far from his ribs! That is how hunger
Comes so close to education.

Oh, for a word on your knees,
To bounce—young, young rays!"
The infrangible is flocking to our head—those words
To which we ran and then from hid.

Here come the wives with sheep in their ears
One stands sick on silver heels,
Like a question unasked, a question that asks
Too much.

And all they say: "We follow the crashes
From shore to shore—

Everything that breaks of terror
Breaks and is whole again
Never to become
Like once-loves become acquaintances,
Truly erect hardware in a dune."

AUBADE

Like a totem of birds, every last one
understood
distinct, built with openly identical
hands;

Hair blew into my mouth when I laughed:
an angle where briefly the gold
mimesis of inedible worms
was hid.

A rifle of Aristophanes,
a butt of Rilke,
the mane of Rintrah,
all kept under the drum pillow,
bluff grass,
while dribbling clouds
roll . . .

"This mirror deprives the face of love—"

The earliness of the bird
that told me, in my red-faced
dynamism, a categorical
uprising
sun . . .

New mobilities, suit up in armor of birds—
stand and test:

"The shield of the heart is the heart—"

Beak—open and close,
open and close,
I count two points of an ungorgeable star—

LADY FOOL

This helium—a fighting voice—promise this—
the old lady said, wires doubling wildly overhead.
Promise is a flock of stairs, which secures salts and buoys in the
   sun these flagrant steps.
In fits—this stamping on—lady in the sun,
headed, like summer's bound feet, straight for the sun. Your sun
   is the hat
and, as your hat, a way of staring
into its widening brim, friend of the castles crumbling all along
the trim. Honey tows from lips of the trim and, as though all
her features by one clockwork step
to their catty-corners morph, a daisy nose ends up where one
   would have sworn was a wart.
Volition is turning our face to some
essence, and waters, too, mount with every resemblance:
These roll in one and bruise the gulls, further in embrace than
   poets, themselves
rolling in the quicksand sun.
Night stamps, finger licks her mummy curls:
Something fumes on a ripple, just one stair—
and something wins—lights rubbed raw of joints
seen as through ruins.

SPARROW

This was more like the atmosphere
had been pinched, whose chirp was an unexpected gust
in a harmonium enough
to break all that high horse talk
that curdles the atmosphere. While centaurs ate

grass and hurdled epitaphs, that chirp
in the midst did change one of us.
'Twas clawed out in a feeling's flock
'Twas 'couraged by the tall grass
Did you not catch it?

It is enough to gather at your age
It is enough to note just what was said
that provoked the Alps and co. to rage.
Tomorrow's eye must follow up and sew along
range; but can it sleep
the crazing off tops of trees?

Just one eye as yours could be enough—
one for six moons that surround
the mind's water birth, while a lily on its cot
bloated, lapses. Sparrow, here again! Countless
consuls, tower and luff but the world
will size down to a restless heart—

To the one note that repeats itself and is all.
To the note one repeats to one's self and all.
To the one line pissing itself into flight.

Metaphor is elsewhere, a jewel resulting in the snout of a pig.
Sparrow, here—nearly unresting thing
which always seems suddenly
never to have left my mind. Because you will so easily disappear,
I think of you as infinitely near.

II

NEWS

A coop of one demon that meant
no harm, rode me perfectly until the morning. Flip, cupid
eyelid—

o

From the first, hot bell of June, he wiped his plate with the skin-
bag of a dove—the dove was full of chimes of mice . . . & the mice
were full with clueless abysses which had their bones collapsed
. . . oh-collapsed until the dove's eyes popped & the plate grew
very white.

o

Was he sick? The rainbow arches
a bit of glitter and he coughs—a little, fitting glory, purple
morns, beheadingly long.

o

Intact, there, like a face from which the plaster of a letter's
irrepressible envelope has been carefully peeled, even those who
did not know they loved her, knew when she left them: their
bodies were crippled but their faces were traveled and glowing.
All warred so poorly in her white noise, then with a uniquely
laxative look one said it a hundred pines can't cram this eye but
a human at an acre even gouges my peace of arc.

o

Today the slowest animal leaves the drawer, but letters will fly back, école! For this he attends only to sing:

Worlds gone rabid!/ Gather and touch my/ lockjaw—now—/ because/ tomorrow I'll lift this ahh-purple/ ban & lay this cripple at the waterfall.

o

And to the lightning foot, my foot quick to sympathize, they chained a pine 20-foot long and gave me a shove toward the 1,000 clouds.

o

Upward and edward and edward and onward—barefoot (in God's thin skin over a mountain, to meet his love), love's shoe a small fluid skid of scorpions.

o

No matter how convinced I am by the image of myself in weakness leaking from the stronghold of my own demonic persuasion, there is simply a promise and that I must keep to myself. How the substance of my smiles often dropped, bursting the welt of each will, seven promenades below, among broken horses, asleep on this radical bunk, not a virgin tint to darken the work of the idolator.

o

So homely that it seems in every effort of innocence I have been
(for all my faults my joys also retard me) grazing off the soles of
evil.
And they slap me, I tell them,
in many fluent directions, even the polite leaf, for my inmost
face of leaves is like
a plane in the empty-handed.

o

Reek rat ampled cheeks this is both running a fat bruise-coloring-
tome.

These meddlesome flashes! If only I could stand this/ parrot in
this/ pan.

o

What I intend, through the fat poised-out tongue and the cut-outs
of friends—
for any can pierce the height I win in walking—
to the right I bend a new timber arrow and yearn—inerts, rats
and all advisory hearts don't follow.

o

Honor of what I have been even if in one moment only, even if that
moment has been flattened by some present, overweight nostalgia
or some imaginative formation that my flying belonged to then.

Now that is yours, for spitting millions on the pageant the street
in which all words are one, as naturally the light lows
numbly, with millions, but particularly, with the footmen at the
rainbow: they double what you leave there, for they are actually
children, standing—one on top the other . . . axles blowing, a full
ground on their lips.

o

A tough skin flies off the stables. The tarmac grins, through the
spider's thong. Then how should one with no enemies be so afraid?
Miles part, she is polite, parting the backfire's hair through an
eidolon hairpiece on tour, to absorb more cud from this upstart
burning. He says there is
another form of happiness, a ring around some dying head in
which his
horses run, before I see the grass and lose it;
until the overwhelming feast is just a tiny teaching broom.

CROWN THE WORDS

A little water, salt, and we'll drown out presently.
We'll crown the words in the next world:
Our word is good, our valence gold.

A vale is a farewell with water running back
to it. A valise a small piece
language banged up in our carousel's

first-love shape. Miss, your valise!
But we're running, outrunning our say—
wave-mouths foaming the hard-pressed

secrets of feeling feeling. Sir, your signature!
We're breathless, the name falling way
behind the hand, the hand a vine wrapping,

over-running. We'll traverse death ungrounding,
rename it quietus, seal it green.
We'll find less termly limits than these.

APPROACHING A MOON-EYED GUARD

How did you come to such a fierce trembling,
to a knotted head? Your eye will

thread tears no more, a doubt tall
even to the angelic. Where's your spool,

moon-eyed doe?
Where is your illumined bouffant?

(..............................)

The wrecked earth sums up
as poorly, after—

You have listened too deeply,
sunk your dewclaw too deep

in the loose pyramid of lost belonging.
You learned where the eye turns too slowly

on its glossy axis,
it is impossible to take your face
into your own hands

without it crumbling. To your heart's content
you've devoted yourself by a thread
to what's just beyond.

When did your pure
intent become ruinous?

(...............................)

SNAIL

Tracks laid down with dawn,

Pace at one with the bride, the runs

Train as long as the aisles of the garden

(One, two, opal grip is milked;

Foot sells galavanter's silk)—

Only every other pause is a swing out black,

Black like rubber curls of the awaited telephone.

When it rains again, you don't answer.

In your modesty, there is a castle—the apex of which

Is the door to your youth. And though

It rains like a beggar at that door,

You've sealed the letter with your foot

For the door it has a slot—and still, your eyes

Bloom each penny trip into the sun

You smooth out. You move in slow ripples, a wave that

Left the sea and from the shore took

A heavy shell as echo and memento.

In circles you go, as if writing a poem

About the sun, or considering what you could

Become. "It was no one," you insist, then curl

To sleep like a fist. Then your eyes

Become microscopes for stars which seem each

A pin in understanding—gold, in a grenade—

SONNET

Worms you know
my history of loose beginnings,
tacked because there is no esteem at the root
for sadness, since flowers focused us

One is pushing long-honed claws of pineapples
to come out through shouldertops,
hills and sea-breast
swells: this one smells of mermaid hair,
fair warning

I am rounding them up
in useless armor
to an old tune

Sharp play pierces home
Glitter in the gills of hills

A TIGER IS GETTING MARRIED

Some were invited; you are
to imagine:

a tiger's wedding—which it was,
you were involved—

is the rain alone and sun,
alone to be imagined.

Alone as pure. Rain, the veil
to a round glowing face

and all the attending faces below.
Oh the streaming,

every color a lace before the eyes.
Carry that train!

But it slips between the fingers,
diamonds.

No groom in sight,
which reminds me the clouds

kindly fled. To not go blind,
so close at the kiss,

there was no kiss at the tiger's wedding,
(some were diamonds,

others pelted)
which is the rain alone and sun.

No one cried, no one forgotten,
imagine that—

a tiger's wedding involving the
stripped and pure,

and yours, a singular absence.
Lates grate, only water

flashes against the sun's eyes
like a veil.

Watch, these bald patches
by morning will be lemons.

IRIS

Here's the one, the unbudded, single stalk, of which our first glimpse and instinct to grasp it are almost synchronized. We want right away to take hold of it between forefinger and thumb and wield it like the too-deeply green-dipped paintbrush it resembles. The wrist aches to hold and flex with it, a newly handled thing, to air-stroke a crescent *n*, a crescent *u*, a swirl, a figure-eight, and this playful act of no consequence is a privilege to anyone who beholds the iris, painter or no. Try a loose comma or a flowing *S*, a tadpole or upside down teardrop— yes! Like a conductor, you may gesture all this with your back to us: with a zip-zap of your vert baton, thrusting and high-strung the heads are off, furiously bowed. A race not unlike the heart's, emoting in place, yet backdropped now with the vase that calls us to return its slender scroll—without orator still—yet to be spurred fully from other flowers, until the head mouths and the flower speaks—then what it says is still wholly unbelievable. The iris fumes purple, returned center stage, and stuns us with its opening petals: three purple-dressed women dipped back by their green-armed partners. It seems we have arrived at the end of some sensuous and resplendent dance! The end but as they say the fireworks: petals each midribbing with a yellow gold streak as though light were coming off a sword which turns invisibly deeper and deep into the sacred stalk and sends the fresh purple blood up brimming to the petal edges of the delicate.

MOTH

Out of all I scoped for most
was the surface of night,
to eke one out of two, twin infinities.
Night's lapel-blown lava-colored clue made me
come to—
(*from where a fragrance rose,*
a reasoning just under the nose):
I said to the flame, with intrigue
at its stationary flight, I'm
not like them—the other moths
don't stay the conversation, jarring off
like staples in a materializing
whistle. Not like them—in flowers as in indices,
demanding to be buried with
their answers. Do I look to you
to be correcting an approach
to love? Fear is an obsession too.
And what did you say then
when I believed the secret had
been waxing like moon moss between us,
in a voice fresh as baptismal splash—
the ample bodied pause was not
what singed, but just the way
things are here, then flown, then up in arms,
then wings, then flames—
You said, "If I could tell you
I would not be so warm"—
You said, "It was that I did not catch."

The broom falls from her arms—
The dancer sputters from honest sleep,
 "How weak these arms! Like reins stripped
From my pale thighs.
The city looks an hourglass, though pulverized!
I am sure to be strewn first and wide
By the senses' gravities
While peas neck and neck
Bolt the sun;

Children bowl over a drugged green, each blade they press
Cricks up after them, halt!
Whose nature is still in nature sealed—they do not guard
It as though a scarcity.
Do not confront me piqued in synch,
My vision all vast on air:
Denial oils the loins,
My savings become my leech."

HOME STATE

What will come so soon to my
Door with a dandelion
For a knob, when asleep from all sides
I am a horse about to be braided,
Asleep in the shattered pajamas of man.
I sat by the pea, a world in the moss:
The sun rose, the day
Was toast: It began, lit down, with running the soft moss
Out of question, and stirring the good walls in
To where I sat.——One still ties his hat to a worm from his home
    state.
Few affections I've left, he said—a breath perfectly folded,
Though that, to some of my peers,
Is the crop of pure pacing. A glass elevator stalls at the groin,
A horizon falls like a tree
Into place, but if I think of everything I cannot hate
If I think of everything I know there isn't evil
Trees of a clearing
Small of a vase

* * *

One night, opening in foil
seven oxen stars pull apart—
one night, one even says hope—
I beat into his chest a call,

into the red rotundas of his chest.
But no one can
hold a hope so long—there's relief.
("Even from passion?" ask the eucalyptuses agog
with your passing.)

The leaves buckle;
the backdrop befriends blunt night;
halt, a knock for the clown—
his mat is round again; halt,
from hard earth throbs a finger lifts
a dew in which
a clean pigeon hangs.

***

While ants were at homes—
Some larger, eyes of racoons, dens
Crammed of crumb,
Others modestly arraigned—
I became a different person,
I can't talk with my children.
I'm not wearing my own clothes.
Wearing my wife's glasses.

You want to pour it blind
To the vast company whose obsessed ablution
Rewilded her eyes.
Top button drops by,
The ceiling bows: that is the night
That pencils in
Hiding, the wanted forever.

But even if encyclopedic periphery were impeached of tapestry
And touch confirms: her eyes—in one
Black nipples splash and in one an alm ball bursts
Amassing down a tangent green, bled to your only likeness
A fact not hiding
But visited by every hidden—
Light as the tangent touching a leper.

III

TUMBLES

All night at my station, my cake-lit foundation totters—like a hat approached by autumn. Ablutions of slitherers-by preoccupy, and the lovelorn grapes must be shaken. Till hollow and evergreen, till Twin, till my horse alerts me of her arrival, its neck is a cannon loaded with pearls. Giant, protect me from the peculiar cliff her notice is, when vibration takes a sudden solo. I am dashed like the giant pearl or the honest tumbleweed—over cliff, into sea, so exposing the foundation's arc. So a bee, dozing like an unpowdered mole on the chin of a tulip, flies to her without waking.

The birthmark of one twin and the seizure in the prefix the other got seeing it expand in her eyes: ah! They built an electric arc, like the instep of Rosanna, over the desert that was their stage. Not the stage, but who they set before themselves, on cauliflower thrones, crowned by fake flowers (I., A Hovering; "Prologue to a Twin Decalogue"). The places moved around like lightning, that drool of storks presaging babies and laughter like burst water balloons.

RAR and RAR I repeat myself—hard raindrops stop my ears. Twenty nights, twenty chapters of headstones and clapping, anything we easily could split in two. But the essence of us twins is nothing if not an epistolary grey. Have you tried to crush one voice into a powder or drown it in oil? It becomes a mont of diamond: then, in its likeness, hail trods the pools of oil at its base, surmounting neatly, as in a double wedding cake. What startles are the pigeons within this harmony debuted, this matter twice over but clear as the combo-bell rung when children are priesting high in a kind of trouble and laughing too near each other to hear.

Multiply white at the copy shop, give thanks to the buffs who propagate your lie. There, a milli crushifacts, shape-shifting a milli ways, pass before an owl with a sartorial eye. Beneath that eye, three tatted drops of milk garner prized sympathies of the moon. To pass and counterpass, never to see it shut! Here is an instant prism inhabited by the other's grand personality. We copy the day long, there we powder young blushers. We boast the one silk nick in this whole molestation of eternity—

See her fingertip's spilling scarfettes, commencing a procession: our muted fanfare for the shy.

The prophecy was also a flourish at the base of the spine, the tail of foxiness boggling the airs of men. The length of your wandering could fit on a pin, so closely do you circle love. At the doorbell sore, pushing for the crowning of abandon. Twins! A beryl show of night and many eager hands, waving from the dollhouse window, lowering a constant tear. Heard a wee music of tiny organs playing fire. Then saw the tiny players themselves drop, blindfolds in a flood.

Twin spoke just once, like a stain. The members wondered at the puddles, saying No No No to a quiz in any other language. What brings salt to the rims of eyes, to the noble, spiral notebooks? What compelled the more privy side of the coat to climax in the grapevine and to reserve that right? The walled cries stopped, for shame, for shame they fell prey to their own musical attention.

To the carnival, in pajamas and toilet paper curls by a billow held. To only kiss and pet in the tree's long shadow, that counts! Our maidenhair whims may well rot in labor, picked sweet off the spine, our son-of-a-cloud. But who wretched a final arrow in collaboration? World-builder, grandmaternal, smilette where children are: Gather these roots in the street and fly these birds from the trees.

No more, younger brothers, do corners call us to one home. Yet we freshen at each offering: the new floss Magellenic millimeters and yoke the royal rope. And we admit murderous nostalgia. In my toast I say I shall and do or I am no thug, with this glass the shy come to; to conquer deer in front, a few doll smiles in the grocketing grass . . .

Obscuring is ambition, bold only among chess pieces. In that zone where talent isolates each I can taste—shavings of calf tongue. In the carcass of old embarrassments, I am still purling an awning for the barefoot Twin. There is so much to see and it is confusing to miss nothing and no one—but in exchange, for the least rung, there is the insulin of the garden and the petal at her chin.

SWEET GUTS

Cock-colors freak and strew. From every indication
is the razing of our perfect ship—
who the rib and what the bore

on a purple petal of the sea?
We'll wooly a way back by wording innards out: to us some
growth is on, on a raised brow, steepled
in misty towels as before in place

of place. All flame is one mane retired on our thimble—
a gesture nobody can measure.

One day I will be able, that is, I will spit out the snake the skin
don't follow. Behind some green-backed diary.

For our steps, strew us petals in glass that
make us wince, "Sweet guts,

O rose-rimmed spectacle!"
And all that we can, in turn, we'll cram,
in whispers, legit through a ventricle.

A RACE

In the lap of the guest so fast,
in the burlap sack of heaping sugars
a crow tied to a fox.
The tusks of dusk snapped
in pepper and a flash of hay.
A hill rolled to the door and knelled, Here, on green knees!
Each mirrored in its spoons of moons, over a shoulder
what it sought:

Thoughts that bind when I run, said the fox,
with pearls for balls; that blind
when a familiar comes, wending from sides
for hitching and nurturing like a fast
friend, with only glows for eyes, like the wicks of crows.

Tendons couple
in a crimson stream and the popped collar moon hums
everything that a morning
will read aloud: too loud, too clear!
I'm on sour breath stilts, said the crow,
to read waters with fury.
Everything that means a happy pauper's emptying or being
driven in such a fashion
as the Great Pollution created by masters to bring
a more certain nature out of its beloved hiding
though it rises only in hairs and moves with friction for a crown
and stands to know so little of what is left
even as day clarifies these white crows the deaf
with dreaming stuff.

APPROACHING A GNAT-EYED NOVICE

If in jugular dark you were treading
flooded patches of melon and cauliflower,
groping for a knuckled banister,
       or you were listening

through deafening curtains of a waterfall
to only your failings,
as if there were no choice,
       no other opera,

then one gnat will be a threat,
one gnat—and its politics, full-blown
but encapsulated, looming yet
       inconspicuous as roses within
       roses.

It will be dark spittle of a rant
(flown over redheads of roses) you can't
follow or muster; over
the patted soil of goodbyes,
never touching down, never gaping,

       Look down—it's futuresque,
       the patted soil

It flies, a speck of you once
recklessness, a seed fighting the creep wind
in the flowerbeds of your headroom.

PRESSED SEAT (NUN'S BUNS)

Butterflies in a gag of buns, in a cool scream,

ganging in one sleeve, finely dusted and paper-thin—still on the tailor's

mannequin. Tiny, black threads show,

conservatively snipped. We must be quiet, not helix any wind—
There are

so many soldered pins—

Four brown wings titter (under some dead leaves) tutelage. And not stop.

Now into a clearing they go, to spindle in the sun

with the mutts. The tree that follows in mercy,

in clear blood falls—The waiter that slides beneath, with crisp cuffs.

Now we must think of everything, the lunar calendar stippled in their trim.

Mustn't babyfatten even a tic of volume, my whole happiness

rises on one breath, on a tossed plate and flashing

its hills and garnishes of bilge.

BRASIL

Left a hole on fire agony or was it the sun
on the banks and near duets?
Eagles with the white wine of the sun
clink and spill, tall
grass over head and heels
. . . Space of hell: shy, inscribed already
but alone—I think I can be that

again, a new hole in the ongoing flute.
In a leap, the country glows—to hone
the fate that wonder exacts,
to go netted through that much,
so heavy as paperweights angels land
square on chaparral nerves.
And since names must give in spades,
out of sorts like these, your reactions
may swell great fountain lips—
a promise that a wish will purge
or pennies caravan the safe
return hearts cross.

BALLAD (STORK DROPPINGS)

The spring storm and the scree
—All loosely crawl into some growth.
But lightning

was for the stork—
a sign of distress, a fatal, drool-etched
SOS . . . Poor, dutiful beak.

Now down the riverbasket goes in marble!
And the drain, so stern.
("All blue weave and vein.")

Sisters of one stair: Heel, heel,
heel around the crossword mold: Though names spread
across our arms,

thunder builds up the sleeves
to gather all in a sense, like edible flowers.

BANANA

The sunbeam is first redder than crash,
Then a yellow, loud and dumb.
And if there is a nose it is soft-shaped
In the business of still-young foes:
The skin dangles from your hand,
Leading comedian, o kingpin with a punchline,
Who finds the fruit is laughable (as we do) and creates
All the to-do, then slips on the lit step up?

Delight is near you, a limp epaulette.
A chunk gleams in your hand: the edible guts of geodes!
A dollop of wet polar bear fur, a fur beneath
The skin! Reversible, like a curse, a logos,
Children's children,
Pounding bright on the sleeve.

ELMER'S WINTER

A clear chariot for all purposes is racing
To the sad man,
Since winter like a white horse kicked in
Letting no one (inches, inches) in—

Any moment—it makes repeated stops
Pulling out the roots
Caught in its wheels:

"Since
We don't know the occasion
Of our say, it's best we save those
Roots for our bouquet.
The horse will whip around our say,
Foam flings oblong from its lips."

A somber fist flowers around a yawn.
In the passing park, busts are roving
In first
Impressions
And feelings captured on a mug.

"Nothing is taken from us
Save in winter rest and then,
Like a glue bottle's milked blossom
From our grips.
The rest, bundled in white, drifts."

"That crown of crows on the boughs,

Fully articulate;
And that clear chariot, cracking the
Bird-bones of firs, gears shifting into
Trinity under their hats."

YOU KNOW ME FROM HERE

It comes familiar by
surprise, to set the chequer-
work of your nesting
in the least places—
dry and dire and gossamer broken
elbow-deep in the blowhole
The great sucks

rhyme when you hear it
—Not the will scalping the waters, not on sobered
cubes of horse-drawn breath to a
bloodless roof. The path onto you sharp—
It comes familiar and refreshed
with little nudes
to mind, just the birdbath

that needs the bird
beyond hands to judge

***

Heroics—it balls all heads to one capital: birth.
Who cares if its freedom is ugly, all are bleeding—
Thus is a standard almost cruel to hold up,
Except that you, by one factory,
Neither man nor woman, upheld it, sucking
Hands to head—
Hands to head, protection's cloud:
It rotates to an ornate tiff
An element of children oned to yourself, carved
With golden rolls—
They shift, hem excrement and sour stilts, slow,
Like a walk along the shelves.
On one shelf sits a face pocked
With soil, now goldenrod,
Pivot to a will:
"They rang on every tier, jus' like that,
The rainbow's clot of what I seen. Cred to the bun
You are building to index force
Where a great white flies."

ACKNOWLEDGMENTS

I am grateful to all the editors of the following periodicals, in which versions of these poems appeared: *Barrow Street*, *Bat City Review*, *Better: Culture & Lit*, *Boston Review*, *Denver Quarterly*, *Everyday Genius*, *Fence*, *Guernica Magazine*, *High Chair*, *Literary Imagination*, *The Paris-American*, *PEN Poetry Series*, *Poetry*, *Tin House*, and *The Winter Anthology*.

I am indebted to the friends and teachers who have inspired and encouraged me with their attention and example, and especially to Christopher Roberts for his immeasurable support as a careful and demanding reader of these poems. Thank you forever to Amaranth Borsuk, Missy Mazzoli, and Beau Shaw for their special powers of encouragement, and a deep dent of thanks to Kristen Gleason to whom "Tumbles," my portion of our ongoing collaborative poem, is dedicated. For their generous support, special thanks to Paulo Britto, Kevin Fathi, Paul Haller and all at the San Francisco Zen Center, Edward Hirsch, Christine Hume, Genine Lentine, Phillis Levin, David Mikics, Brigit Pegeen Kelly, Stephen Yenser, and especially to Reed Wilson, who was there at the beginning; and to the MacDowell Colony, Fulbright Program, and Poetry Foundation, for honoring me with the gifts of space and time in which to write. A synchronized wave of thanks to Lynn Buckley for this beautiful cover. The ultimate thank you to Joshua Edwards and to everyone at Canarium for making this book actual and yours.

Farnoosh Fathi is the author of the poetry collection *Great Guns* (Canarium, 2013), editor of *Drafts, Fragments and Poems: The Complete Poetry of Joan Murray* (NYRB Poets, 2017), and founder of the Young Artists Language and Devotion Alliance (YALDA). She lives in Brooklyn, New York.